HOW TO START AND RUN AN IT CONSULTANCY BUSINESS

Disclaimer

Contents

About the Author

Srikanth Merianda is a developer, entrepreneur, and investor with over 15 years of experience as employee and employer. He has worked for Convergys, Nortel Networks and Blackberry as Software Engineer, Project Manager, Architect, and Implementation of mission critical projects.

Srikanth has successfully started multiple IT Consulting Firms, Business process outsource Firms, and Mobile Apps development firms. He guided these companies through start-up, survival, turnaround and growth phases.

Besides setting up firms, Srikanth also provides IT consulting service to mission critical integration projects as well as technical and cost assessment for Software projects. With his wealth of experience, knowledge, and expertise, he has provided technical and business consulting services to companies and some have gone to gross over $1 million in their first year of getting consultancy services from him.

Srikanth is a passionate programmer and an enthusiastic learner of all things technology. He constantly looks for ways to make work and life easier with the tools provided by technology. He holds a Bachelors Engineering degree in Computer Science and a Master of Science in Computer Science from the Mississippi State University.

www.consultingopportunity.com

Introduction

Do you want to break out of the corporate life and do something that you love? Well, who doesn't?

Many professional working men and women dream about starting a consult-ancy business they can call their own. After all, it is a great career path - you hang a shingle, attract clients, are your own boss, do great things, and ultimately, make big buck!

However, consultancy, contrary to popular belief, is not as easy, sexy or glamorous as most people perceive. In fact, it is a lot harder than you may think and requires more than just a business card or organizational ability. In addition, you can most definitely expect a few hurdles in your path. This raises the question, how can you successfully start and run your consultancy business? Well this is what we shall discover in this eBook.

First off, being a consultant, your job is to consult your clients - it is pretty much as simple as that. There is no secret that makes a consultant better than another. However, a constant drive and passion for excellence, and not to mention, being knowledgeable about the subject you are consulting in is what differentiates a good consultant from a bad one. Unbelievably, this makes a *huge* difference!

In these modern times, just about anybody can be a consultant and all it really takes is discovering what your particular gift is. If information technology is your forte and you like to keep up with the latest hardware and software information - that changes almost daily - then you should have no trouble working as an IT consultant. You will, though, need some assistance to start and run your consultancy business, and this is exactly what this eBook will provide.

Moreover, you can also find a lot of resources to help you save time and/or automate the process.

Please visit http://www.consultingopportunity.com/ and send all suggestions to info@consultingopportunity.com.

Srikanth Merianda, BE, MS

Chapter 1 – What is Information Technology Consulting?

In today's business climate, having business consultants of all varieties is increasingly important. They offer high -impact advice, backed by years of exper-ience, for busin-esses of all sizes. In fact, they prove to be a cost-  effective solution to hiring full-time, pricey staff.

Although an on-site IT department or professional is essential for many types of large or-ganizations, the truth is that even small start-ups need to access the kind of advice and skills offered by information technology experts. And this is where information technology consulting can prove useful.

IT consultants, who take the form of either a business that handles all your information technology needs or an individual professional offering independent consultancy services, can step in and effectively fill technology gaps within a business at a fraction of the cost of having a full staff.

How Hiring an IT Consultant Is Good for Business?

Saves Money

The services offered by IT consultants are available on a contractual or hourly basis. Depending upon the needs of the business - whether they require one-time java programming or regular Windows administration work - they may find themselves constantly hiring an IT consultant on a regular basis or for short-term projects.

Both of these options will allow businesses to effectively control the cost of their IT solutions. And since they hire outside the company, the fees and taxes associated with hiring a staff member can be avoided, further reducing the cost of having an IT expert on board.

Saves Time

With IT consultants, businesses can streamline their operations. For instance, if the server is overloaded, employees will not be able to communicate and work as effectively as they should. The same is the case with important data, which if lost, could result in costly downtime.

Waiting for a solution will simply worsen the problem and have a negative impact on the business' bottom line. Good IT consultants, however, are on hand at all times and have the ability - and tools - to get their IT infrastructure on track by providing solutions well-before a disaster actually occurs, making them prepared for anything that comes their way.

Increases Productivity

Lastly, the most important thing IT consultancy can do is allow business and their employees to get back to doing what they do best. For most businesses, backing up data or repairing a server is something they can handle on their own. Besides, the internet has an abundance of advice and how-to articles to help businesses stay technologically up-to-date.

However, specialization is essential for good business, and savvy business owners are well aware of this fact. While having cross skills does prove useful, rarely is it a good use of time or cost-effective. Having an IT consultant on board means businesses can rest assured knowing that these professionals will streamline processes to increase productivity, that too, without overtaxing their finances or employees.

Now that you have a better understanding of what is required of you when starting and running an IT consultancy business of your own, let's move on to the next chapter, where you will familiarize yourself with the wide range of benefits of having such a business.

www.consultingopportunity.com

Chapter 2 – What are the Benefits of Starting an IT Consulting Firm?

Do you have a taste for the finer things in life, like champagne, caviar and suave business suits? Perhaps you dream of working from your MacBook while vacationing in Fiji. Alternatively, maybe you just want to give a seminar at a TED conference. Well, the sky is the limit, so go ahead and dream BIG as you will be more likely to fulfill your goals.

Anything can be accomplished as long as you are willing to go the extra mile, and pay the price for it. However, it is also important to understand that luxuries such as these come as a reward for taking risks and overcoming difficulties to run a successful business. And they, by themselves, are not actually the best reasons to start one.

When it comes to IT consulting, you need to know it is a relationship business first, that crosses different types of organizations, that too, in all sizes. Therefore, while being smart and having the necessary professional knowledge is essential, it alone is not enough to succeed!

The question you need to ask is: do you have what it takes to start an IT consulting firm of your own? To help you out, here are a number of reasons why starting an IT consulting business is worth the hard work. If you are able to say, "Hey, that's me!" to all of them, consider yourself ready to take the next step.

Big Paychecks

Once you have achieved a substantial amount of experience in your domain, i.e. Information Technology, your knowledge becomes a valued asset. While you may know this already (of course you do!), what you may not be aware of is that the market for your knowledge is a lot bigger than your current and potential customers.

In recent years, more businesses are using IT consulting as a means to reduce their ever-increasing IT costs. In addition, since hiring an IT consultant does not involve any fees or taxes, as is the case with full-time employees, they are able to enjoy the services of an IT professional for a lower cost.

As a result, you can easily charge anywhere from $100 to $120 per hour for consultation with clients, whether over the phone or face-to-face, once or twice a month, depending on their needs. This, therefore, allows you to add a sizeable amount of money to your paychecks. And the best part of all is there is not a lot of preparation involved, so this proves quite an attractive return on time!

Flexibility & Freedom

 When you successfully establish an IT consultancy business, you become your own boss and have the flexibility and freedom to do what you want, when you want. In other words, you will have the ability to choose the tasks you want to

undertake, clients you want to work for, and when you want to finish work.

This, however, does not necessarily mean you can just work just a few hours every week, and will be still able to take your business to new heights. No, that is not how it works! You need to concentrate on the key areas of your business, and work within these parameters to accomplish your goals.

You do not need to handle every task on your own, though. After all, you are not restricted by process anymore. Hence, when necessary, you can always outsource or delegate the less important tasks to others, while you concentrate on taking your IT consultancy business to the next level.

Love What You Do

When you start your consultancy business, it is obvious that it will be in a field you are passionate about. Your ability to generate revenue will primarily be dependent on the results you are able to deliver. After all, that is what businesses will hire you for in the first place: to come and assess their operations so you can provide them with expert advice to solve their problems, and in turn, improve performance.

Since you love what you do, you will have the enthusiasm and vitality to attract potential clients who would want to work with you. Not to mention, your passion will drive you to make a difference and offer these businesses the value they deserve. By continually adding skill sets or new services, you are bound to rise to the top, and this self-awareness is exactly what you need to make it big in the IT consultancy business.

Stay Up-to-Date

Talking to clients in your space is undoubtedly a two-way exercise. As an IT consultant, your primary purpose is to educate and advise them. However, this, at the same time, will also inevitably provide you the opportunity to stay up-to-date with the latest happenings in the IT industry.

And chances are that you will become familiar with at least one, if not more, unknown perspectives. Therefore, at the end of the day, you get to bring home some food for thought and motivation! Sure, a non-disclosure agreement will require you to keep the received information secret, but those discussions would certainly improve your understanding of the space you are navigating.

Speak Your Mind

Being an IT consultant does not mean you are an employee of the business you are working with. Whether you have your own consulting firm, or even if you work for one, you are considered an IT consultant and not an employee when you go to your clients to help them out.

Since the field of consultancy, regardless of the area, requires the professional to speak their mind freely, you will be able to tell the company what they are doing wrong, and how they can go about solving those problems. Besides, that is exactly what you are paid for, right?

Remember, this is an extremely important trait and there are many people who are afraid to speak their mind in the corporate world. When you speak your mind, you are helping the company who hired your service to do even better, so never shy away from saying what you are thinking, especially if it is in the best interest for the company.

Effective Communication

One of the best things you will learn as an IT consultant is to communicate effectively. You will not be spending most of your time working in an office, and you will be aware of the fact that your gig still is not steady. Hence, you will need to keep providing results to stay relevant in the IT consultancy market.

However, providing results alone is not enough. You will, in fact, also need to show these results to your clients and this can be possible through meeting, reports, phone calls, emails or any form of communication you think would be appropriate and useful.

When your clients will hear from you regularly, they will realize that you are working on what they asked, and producing the desired results to make their processes more efficient. As soon as you stop communication, though, they will think you are not taking the job seriously, and could end up being fired.

By starting your IT consultancy business, you will be able to polish your communication skills by a great deal, which let us face it, is important regardless of what you are doing in life.

Problem Solving

As with any other field of consulting, your job as an IT consultant is to identify and solve any problems your clients face. Most of the times, you have a free reign to get this done in whatever way you want, but in some instances clients want the problems to be solved within specific guidelines.

This means you have to think out of the box, which is extremely important for you to learn because it will allow you to solve the most complex of problems with ease, that too, across any industry! With improved problem solving skills, you will be able to tackle anything your client throws your way.

In addition, you can work in any field or industry in the future, as you will know how to adapt to any environment. Moreover, let us not forget that businesses are on the lookout to hire people who can handle just about any problem thrown their way.

And that is about it. These are just some of the many benefits you can reap by starting an IT consulting business. In the next chapter, we will take a closer look at some of the top jobs in the Information Technology industry, and what each of them entails.

Srikanth Merianda, BE, MS

Chapter 3 – Top Jobs in Information Technology

Information technology, also known as IT, is a phrase you

may have heard many times if you ever worked with an IT professional or went to college to educate yourself in the field of comp- uters. IT work-ers are highly spec- ialized in what they do, and are essential to the success of just about every business model.

If a company relies on computer systems to get their job done, it is highly probable that there is an IT team behind it all making sure the machinery is functioning properly. You may wonder, are there any real benefits of being the technological lifeblood of a company?

Excellent pay is one of the many benefits as the requirements of IT professionals has now become vast than ever. In case you are curious about what you would like to do, and how much you will be paid to do it, here are some of the top jobs in information technology you should be aware of:

Data Analyst

Although it might not be the highest paid IT job, the salary potentials of Data Analysts are increasing at a rapid rate. Since Data Analysis is an ongoing process in many businesses, as they translate complex number and data into understandable language, just about any company that is reliant on anything from market research to sales figures will benefit from the presence of a Data Analyst.

According to latest statistics, Data Analysts can earn anywhere from $100,000 to $120,000 per year. A Bachelor's degree is all you need to get started as a Data Analyst, but if you are looking to advance in the industry, a Master's degree is what you should be aiming for.

Software Engineer

One of the most well known IT jobs, Software Engineers are the professionals behind the coding of your favorite applications and websites. However, there is a lot more than just coding involved in Software Engineering. In addition to creating code, Software Engineers also work with various aspects of the technology sector, from marketing pros implementing analytics to optimize or boost their marketing and sales performance to designers iterating their thoughts for a great product design.

Since Software Engineers are capable of handling all of these tasks, it does not come as a surprise that they demand a high dollar. A Software Engineer can earn anywhere from $87,000 to $228,000 per year. To get started, though, a Bachelor's degree in Software Engineering, Computer Science or Information Technology is recommended.

IT Security Manager

The title of this IT job pretty much says it all! It is the job of an IT Security Manager to manage the rules and stances of your company in terms of proper computer etiquette and usage. Besides that, their job also includes analyzing the current security condition of a company and identifying its weak points in order to improve. IT Security Managers, designated within a company, are considered the backbone of the company's security infrastructure.

For this reason, IT Security Managers will often collaborate with Network Architects to ensure the security decisions they make are good ones. These professionals earn anywhere from $101,000 to $125,000 per year. Starting out as an IT Security Manager is primarily dependent upon the amount of experience you have in the IT world, coupled with a Master's or Bachelor's degree in Computer Science or Information Technology.

Database Developer

Behind every successful company is a strong database that allows them to securely store all of their important data and information. Database Administrators and Developers are the professionals who not only create databases according to the size and requirements of a company, but also work on its upkeep to ensure the database continues to function well.

Some days, Database Developers have to work behind a computer, whereas on others they may need to communicate with other individuals to resolve any issues in the database. While this job is quite similar to IT Security Managers, the main difference is that Database Developers focus on the security of the databases rather than other aspects of a company's IT infrastructure.

Database Developers can make anywhere from $85,000 to $103,000 per year. A Bachelor's degree in Data Analysis, Information Technology or Computer Science is what is required to get your career started as a Database Developer and Administrator.

Network Architect

Just as if an Architect interprets the wishes or wants of a client or developer into a business or residential property, a Network Architect interprets the wishes or wants of a company on the technical front in order to build the best possible computer infrastructure. This will includes things as straightforward as moving a company from all MAC to Windows to more complex tasks like ensuring the security infrastructure of the company provides adequate security and confidentiality of an employee's personal records.

A Network Architect earns anywhere from $100,000 to $150,000 per year. If you are looking to break into the field and earn some experience, a Bachelor's degree in quantitative fields like Engineering or Mathematics should suffice. However, you should also have some programming experience in different languages, especially HTML.

Chief Information Officer

Undoubtedly, the highest paid IT job around, a Chief Information Officer is the highest position you can go in IT within a company. These people are usually give less task work, and are more actually there to ensure the vision of the company is upheld, and continues to do so.

Unlike Chief Technology Officers, who are present to ensure the development and coding side continues to grow and expand with the technological advancements of a company, CIO's deal with the behind-the-scene problems to ensure what's happens on the front end is working efficiently and safely. A Chief Information Officer can earn anywhere from $175,000 to $219,000 per year and a considerable amount of experience is necessary to work at this position.

Chapter 4 – Steps to Start and Operate an IT Consulting Firm

It is no secret that starting and operating a company is a monumental task. It requires hard work and is fraught with countless risks that can threaten your company's competitive edge, financial success and even survival. Not only will you need to secure financing, but also purchase the required equipment and find a location for the business, all of which takes both time and money.

Launching an IT consulting firm is no different. Apart from all the aforementioned things, it is also essential to possess sound technical ability in the field of specialization, strong communication and negotiation skills, as well as the ability to identify and rectify any issues that may come up. While the process can be overwhelming, there is no doubt that running an IT consulting business can be a rewarding experience.

However, most entrepreneurs who start out in the IT consulting field end up making mistakes which set the stage for future problems, and that's when things begin to go wrong. These, though, can be easily avoided! To ensure you successfully start and operate an IT consulting firm, you can call your own, we have outlined the steps you have to take to get there. So, let us get started, shall we?

Step #1: Decide What Skills You Plan to Consult With

The key to being a successful consultant, regardless of the field, is to decide the skills you are going to market.

Preferably, you should have some type of networking, programming skills or other IT skills that are in demand, otherwise entry into the market could prove challenging. There are a wide range of skill niches which are in demand by businesses that do not have the time or skills to train their employees.

The difference between running an IT Consultancy business using your own skills, against finding clients to send multiple resources to solve a problem or complete a project is that you would be able to make a margin of about $10-$50/hr per resource. The skills that are highly needed of technical people are developers in Java, .NET, Big Data, Database, eCommerce, Database, Hybris, Pega, etc.

Step #2: Decide Your Expected Income

Getting a client prior to starting out is one of the best ways to launch your IT consulting business. Nowadays, it is quite easy to get part-time work to assess whether if it is worth going full-time. By doing so, you will also get a clear idea of the kind of income you are capable of earning once you go out on your own. The most important thing you will have to determine is what you are worth to a client.

For instance, if you get a client who needs 10 Java developers to work on a 6-month project and you have a $10 margin between the billing rate and payment rate, you have the opportunity to make $104,000.00 in margin for the 6 months while the consultants are working at the client's location on your company's behalf. This one project can itself lead to multiple new opportunities.

As an added bonus, you can sign up with a company that I can refer to get daily requirements by email just go to

www.consultingOpportunity.com/SupplierReferral and fill up your information and you can get on the Vendor list of one company that chooses to call you back.

This will get you started with at least 5 to 10 contract job openings per month in the US and Canada. If you can successfully hire someone at a lower rate, you can submit him or her to the Vendor /Client at a higher rate and keep a good margin for yourself.

Step #3: Prepare a Business Plan

Some IT consultants spend a great deal of time in preparing a great business plan, but fail to generate any billable income. Therefore, it makes sense to hold off on crafting that plan, at least until you are able to rake in some revenue. In fact, the perfect time to develop a business plan is when you have loads of work to do, and feel that you have reached a point where you are starting to turn away business.

So, once you have made it to this point, take a few hours out of your day to sit down and work on creating a business plan for the next two to three months. When you have started to get billing income, you will be able to prepare an accurate business plan as opposed to developing it based on what you think may happen. With a proper business plan in place, you will be better able to run your business.

Step #4: Get Started on Your Business Housekeeping

When the revenue starts to flow in, you need to think about setting up your business housekeeping. There are several different types of business to choose from, including a corporation, limited corporation, partnership and sole proprietorship. Most entrepreneurs in the consulting business start as a sole proprietor, and change their business entities as they continue to grow. Next up, you will need a business name and a few, if not all, of the following business basics:

- A website

- A business phone number

- Business cards with your contact information

- Business licenses

- Active presence on social media sites (like Twitter, Facebook and Google+)

- Errors and omissions insurance

- A business email address

- Branded invoicing statements and business letterhead (these can also be automated in accounting software or be templates in MS Word)

- A nice, appealing brochure that highlights your business skills and focus

There are also various options available online to get started. All you have to do is go to:
ConsultingOpportunity.com/resources, and research your options

Step #5: Market Your Business for Exposure

As with any other business, you need to market your consulting business to gain exposure and clients. Although word-of-mouth is the easiest way to promote your business, let us face it, which simply is not enough, especially in today's highly competitive market. Attending business meetings and conferences to meet potential clients is perhaps the best way for full-time IT consultants to get out there.

It is also a great idea to hand out your business cards with email and social contact information at local business expos. A giveaway, such as offering four hours of free IT consulting services, can also do wonders. Get potential clients to fill out a form with their information and ask them to drop it in a box. Even if you get 20 responses, you will have 20 potential clients to work with.

Step #6: Handle the Billing Process Diligently

Although many IT consultants hate dealing with billing paperwork, it is of utmost importance to handle it professionally and diligently. For every hour that you work, you should get your clients to sign a statement verifying they have been billed by you for those hours. Then, send invoices to your clients once a month requesting payment for your services.

This will ensure you are paid and do not waste your time on clients that have issues with your work as soon as you hand them a big invoice. While it is quite unfortunate, many clients try to put off paying you if they believe they can easily get away with it. However, by demonstrating your professionalism from the start and billing weekly or monthly, your clients will know your work has value.

Although you can manually do it with MS Word and MS Excel, we use QuickBooks for accounting and invoicing. Here is a link for discounts upon initial use: **ConsultingOpportunity.com/Accounts**.

Step #7: Focus on Meeting Deadlines

Your clients expect you to meet the given deadlines. Therefore, if you come to realize that you may be late in providing a deliverable for any reason whatsoever, you should let your client know about it immediately. In fact, you might even have to negotiate a reduction in fees to accommodate the client. This happens to the best of people, and while it may not always be your fault, you do need to learn how to handle it.

Step #8: Stay on Top of Your Cash Flow

It is extremely important to know exactly what amount of cash you require to keep your business running. This is because if you do not have enough cash to fund your daily operations, your business may be at risk of running out of money, and eventually, hitting a wall. According to some experts, businesses should have at least two to three months of funds to get their business going, whereas others believe having 6 months worth of cash in the bank is necessary.

The situation will vary between businesses, but it makes sense to start accumulating cash whilst they are still working a full-time job. In this way, you will be able to stay away from cash flow pressures. Moreover, once you have a feel for how much cash you can make, you can determine what amount goes into the bank and what can be used immediately.

Step #9: Establish a Routine to Steer Away from Pitfalls

Consulting is a profitable business as consultants are required in all occupations. Therefore, it is undoubtedly a great way to get self-employed and earn good money, however, it still has its share of pitfalls. How can you avoid them? The easiest way to do so is by setting aside a few hours weekly to review what's lined up for the next week. Here are a few things you should ask yourself:

- How is the cash flow looking for this week and the upcoming four weeks?

- Do I need to address any problems with my existing clients?

- What deliverables am I expected to make for this week?

- Are there any marketing calls or meetings that I need to make this week?

- Should I schedule any critical lunch meetings for the following week?

Step #10: Follow Up With Your Clients

After you have completed a project or task with a particular client, your work does not end there. Get feedback from your clients to make sure they are content with the job you have done. Following up with your clients also shows that you value your client's business. You could even ask them to fill out an evaluation form, as this would give you an idea regarding what they think about your work and which areas you may need to improve on.

The last thing that is important is accounting and invoicing, which can be made easier through manager-approved timesheets. You or your consultants need to send Manager approved timesheets to send the invoice to the client to be paid in time!

Srikanth Merianda, BE, MS

Chapter 5 – Frequently Asked Questions

If you have managed to make it this far, it is safe to say you are genuinely interested in starting an IT consulting firm of your own. However, you might have some questions about the role you will play as an IT consultant and what it takes to leap into this field.

As with any career choice, it can be somewhat challenging to predict what a path in IT consulting will bring you. To help you develop a better understanding of what you are likely to expect, we have presented answers to 10 of the most asked questions about IT consulting:

1. **"What are the educational requirements for a career as an IT consultant?"**

When hiring IT consultants, companies normally look for candidates with a bachelor's degree in computer science, computer engineering, information technology or a related field. While a postgraduate degree is not necessarily a requirement, it can certainly help you move up the success ladder and gives you an edge over the competition in the market.

2. **"What is the average salary for an IT consultant?"**

Since there are many specialties in the IT industry, the salaries of IT consultants tend to vary greatly. In fact, it primarily depends upon what the IT consultant can do as well as how much competition there is for their level of expertise and range of skills. How they charge for their services - fixed fees, hourly rate or daily rate - will also affect the amount an IT consultant can earn.

According to statistics, though, those who are in the early stages of their career can make up to $62,000 per year. However, individuals with 5 to 10 years of experience under their belt bring in around $82,000 on average. Very experienced IT consultants, on the other hand, enjoy larger paychecks of anywhere between $ 118,000 and $133,000 per year.

3. "What is a typical day for an IT consultant looks like?"

Well, there really is not a 'typical day' for an IT consultant and pretty much the same can be said for the entire consulting industry. Most of the days at your IT consulting firm will be occupied with learning and building your network, brainstorming next steps or possible solutions and attending both client as well as team meetings.

Moreover, since you are your own boss, your workdays will not always be the traditional 9 to 5 schedule. You will have the freedom and flexibility to work on your own terms, but that does not necessarily mean you can take off whenever you want, especially when you have just started out and want your business to grow!

4. "How much will I need to travel?"

Traveling is undoubtedly a major part of being an IT consultant, and therefore you can expect to be on the road - or in the air - more often than not. How much time you will spend traveling to different destinations will primarily depend upon on the clients you are working for. However, one thing is for certain: you are going to be on the go to meet your clients on a frequent basis!

5. "Is my role as an IT consultant flexible?"

One of the greatest things about starting an IT consulting business of your own is the flexibility it brings. On average, IT consultants work a minimum of 40 hours per week, but considering the nature of this job, it is not uncommon to sometimes work from home or schedule hours based on client meetings.

6. "What are the different IT consulting roles and titles?"

There are many kinds of IT consultants, and the company's purpose of hiring a consultant will determine the kind of IT consultant they hire. The following are some of the most prominent IT consulting roles and titles:

- Chief Architect, Information Technology (IT)
- Information Technology (IT) Architect
- Senior Software Architect
- Sr. Software Engineer/ Programmer/ Developer
- Software Development Manager
- Information Technology (IT) Director'
- Chief Information Officer (CIO)
- Information Technology (IT) Manager
- Vice President (VP), Information Technology (IT)
- Program Manager, Information Technology (IT)
- Project Manager , Information Technology (IT)
- Information Technology (IT) Manager
- Senior Project Manager, Information Technology (IT)
- Information Technology (IT) Director

7. "What if I am lacking sufficient experience?"

If you are interested in starting your career as an IT consultant, but lack relevant work experience, do not worry - it is not the end of the world! While most companies often look for experienced individuals, you can land an interview by utilizing any related interests, awards, projects or assignments.

You can also gain the experience and skills needed to provide consulting services by working at an entry-level information technology position such as IT technician or computer support specialist. The IT industry is recognized for its fast career development, so rest assured you will not be stuck in the same position for too long!

8. "Should I be taking any specialization courses?"

You can gain an extraordinary advantage over your competition by taking specialization courses as you start your career. In fact, it will also prove useful when it comes to prospecting your own clients. So, what particular courses should you be taking on?

Well, there is a wide range of specialization programs available for individuals who are aspiring to become IT consultants. In addition, whichever you choose to go with, you can be certain that it will provide you with the necessary skills and knowledge to prosper in the ever-changing world of IT.

9. "What kinds of companies are interested to hire an IT consultant?"

There is no definite answer to this question as each company looks to hire IT consultants for their own specific needs.

However, one thing similar is that they require the expertise and skills IT consultants have to offer in order to execute projects or solve problems successfully.

10. "What will my daily responsibilities entail? "

Being an IT consultant, you will have several responsibilities to attend to on a daily basis. While it is impossible to list down all of them, the following are some responsibilities you are expected to take care of:

- Presenting strategies and expertise to clients
- Identifying, developing and implementing solutions
- Effectively communicating with your team and clients
- Traveling to and from client sites
- Designing, installing, testing and monitoring new systems
- Preparing documentation to help clients learn about the system and presenting reports to show performance/results.
- Involvement in sales and support, and where necessary, maintain close contact with clients.
- Diving into the latest industry changes, news and trends.

Now, since you have the answers to the frequently asked questions about IT consulting, you are one step closer to taking your IT consulting business to the heights you - and every other entrepreneur like you - dream of!

www.consultingopportunity.com

Chapter 6 – Commonly Used Terms You Need to Know

Once you become an IT consultant, having multilingual capabilities can prove useful in case are handed an international project. However, what most consultants - regardless of their field - do not expect is that they are required to learn a new second language from the start of their career: *Consultant-ese*.

Yes, you heard just right! Consultants everywhere have created their own dialect, and therefore it can be challenging to keep up if you are unaware of them. Therefore, before you find yourself slack-jawed after hearing any of these terms, study up on the commonly used vocabulary we have listed below, and you will be conversing like a true IT consultant in no time!

- **20,000 feet:** Summary of a situation where only key points are discussed
- **W2:** A salaried employee who is paid on an hourly basis
- **1099:** Those jobs that are performed by a business owner instead of their employees
- **Actionable:** Something that can be done or acted upon
- **At the End of the Day:** A very common term which describes the ultimate or final result
- **Adding Value:** This phrase revolves around the idea of being productive in a positive manner
- **Buy-in:** Consent and/or agreement

- **Buckets:** Refers to groups or categories when talking about a specific project
- **Buttoned-Down:** To be completely and thoroughly professional
- **Case:** A project (also referred to as an Engagement or Study)
- **Commission:** The fee that is paid to for a resource's work
- **Client:** A company looking for consultancy expertise to implement a project or solve issues
- **C2C:** This means that your client deals with your business directly
- **CAD:** Canadian Dollar
- **Deliverables:** Tasks or jobs to be completed
- **Due dil:** Short form for due-diligence
- **Deck:** A slide presentation
- **EOD:** An acronym for "End of Day"
- **End Client:** A company that uses your consulting services and benefits from it
- **Facetime:** Meeting face-to-face or in person
- **F1 Visa:** A nonimmigrant visa for individuals wishing to study in the US
- **H1B Visa:** A nonimmigrant visa that allows US citizens to employ foreign workers
- **Leverage** This is an extremely common term which refers to the use of people, materials, resources or knowledge to achieve what is desired
- **Mission Critical:** A service, product, analysis or concept that is irreplaceable
- **MECE:** Acronym for "Mutually Exclusive, Collectively Exclusive", which means developing communications that address all relevant issues effectively

- **Rock Star:** The top performers of a consulting firm
- **Referral Fee:** A one-time fee that is paid for finding a resource
- **RTR:** Acronym for Right to Represent
- **RPH:** Rate per hour
- **SME:** This important term means "Subject Matter Expert" which refers to the individual you call first when you are unable to understand a specific topic
- **Supplier:** Company that provides consulting services to clients
- **TN Visa:** A non-immigrant status in the United States for Mexicans and Canadians
- **Touch base:** To get in contact with someone, especially with those you haven't talked to in a long time
- **USD:** United States Dollar
- **USC:** United States Citizen
- **Vendor:** A company that gives a job order
- **Value-Add:** Used to describe anything that adds value
- **Workplan:** A set of tasks or schedule for the completion of a project
- **Work Permit:** Temporary or permanent Canadian work visa

Therefore, all you have to do is get yourself accustomed to these commonly used terms, and managing the day-to-day functions of your IT consulting business should not be much of a problem. After all, you will be well aware of the many terminologies that are used in different situations!

Conclusion

And that is a wrap! With that, you have finally reached the conclusion of the eBook, "How to Start and Run an IT consultancy Business". If you information technology is your passion, and you are looking to start your career as an IT consultant, following the steps mentioned in this eBook should help you achieve what you have always dreamed of.

Our resources page will be updated constantly with the tools we evaluate and use for improving our process to decrease time and increase productivity. Please visit our website: http://www.consultingopportunity.com/resources.

For any suggestions please email:
info@consultingopportunity.com and we will review and include all suggestions in our updates, special topics books and website.

Please click the link below to leave a review that would help me improve the book or any part of the book that you feel helped you be more effective.

www.consultingopportunity.com/ITBusiness/Review

Srikanth Merianda, BE, MS